beating the lilies

matthew young

1

First Edition

Cover painting by Matthew Young

I

the shine after the bad

(written at) Kilty's Irish Pub

drops of rain
puddles of pain
hands intertwined
words welded together
heavy thoughts
and a tight nervous
endless pang of
existence has settled
upon this French afternoon
as tears fall from red eyes
onto the pebbled path of Pere Lachaise
and my head starts a-spinnin'
as I drink this pint
and the radio is playing
American tunes
which whirl me back
to you

Paris, France July 4, 2004

ghost dancing

stealth night revolving
around neon orange lights
downtown dances
soft eye entrances
flash bulbs flicker
let us linger in this picture forever
with no cares or worries

you're mine tonight
let's dance
dance into eternity
hearts and souls
intertwined

late night drunken ramblings
sweet haze of hash delighting
the skyline horizon
slumber speckles of twinkling stars
sing to us their ode to joy

heartbeats
rubbing of milky flesh
supple nipples
caress of creamy lips

hold me
kiss me
love me
long into the night

last night in Paris (July 2004)

to be alone
on the river's edge
watching time unfold
into eternity

being eyed by mad bums
softly sipping chilled beer
longing for a stranger's warm hand

mind riding on the metro
to Pere Lachaise
grounding out rhymes of lust
into crowded bars

sedate cemetery
sing to me once more
your song for the seasons

<u>sleep time</u>

the speakers speak softly
hushing a gentle vibe
that's lost in an air stream
which floats by my head
and blindly hits the wall
dispersing into millions
of smaller air streams
who continue the sleepy cycle
until lights burn out
and the carpet sets fire to the sun

10/24/2004

all there is simply is

when it starts burnin'
and the clouds begin grayin'
at the thought of hope
and the dope wears off
and your pockets are empty
all there is
simply is

sing you

I drink you in
and get a hot light
bath in your eyes
waking up next to eternity
with a sun so true
that sings you
sings you
oh-oh

golden fields sway
with stopped motion
echoing whispers
echoing caresses
of us
inside and outside of rhymes
I'll rhyme you
under that moon so blue
then sing you
sing you
oh-oh

I know you
as I come into you
feeling you for all its worth
penny thoughts
which make me into a millionaire
I know you
as you feel for me
feel
free
into
the sea
where the waters
sing you
sing you
oh-oh

diet christ

one whisper echoes
the setting sun

no one hears it but me
no one sees it but you

I pick the loveliest rose from
Shakespeare's garden and
hand it to you

upon seizing it
its reddened hue darkens
and its lush petals
wither and fall to the floor

where they shall remain forevermore

poem for Nick

a shooting star rockets across this chilled out winter sky tonight
sending a solemn message to those watching
those waiting
those searching for an answer
an answer that may bring tears to the eyes
or soft joys to the heart
an answer some may choose to ignore
an answer that may be spoon-fed
to the eagerly awaiting lovers
wondering if their old loves have found
new loves

it's an answer that finds its way to us
someday
somehow
and there ain't no way around it
there's no corners to duck down in
no shelter that keeps it from rainin' down
on our heads
no mask to blindfold us from it

it finds us on a chilled out winter night like this
then disappears forever
leaving its heated trail seared in the depths
of our hearts forever

reality set ablaze

I wish I could change myself
to be the man you
want me to be

I wish I could set the clock on fire
and have you again
have you in my arms again
feel those warm tingles in my soul
when ya kiss my cheek again

I'm dreamin'
I'm lost
my chest aches
as smoker's cough sets in
my memories are set ablaze
by reality
a reality that grows
with every passing second
a reality that ends when you
come home

I'm looking out my window
and your parking space
is still empty

West Chatham St. Blues

a growing world without you
in the real
only a trip that expands
out into the streets

the screeching of your
cat's claws
the cracking open of a
beer
the soft flicker of a lighter
consuming a flame

nervous laughter

sadness bleeds into
the night's silken veil
as you move me into the kitchen
under your sweet summertime spell

night follies

these precious minutes are adding up
and falling down upon other precious
minutes which are no longer precious anymore
but are only ghosts
ghosts that tell stories of time
small artifacts of joy
each wrapped with a glittering
red bow
sealed neatly under a shimmering package
which we can open at Christmas
when the snow ceases to cool
and the fire's warm glow is
extinguished by a lone
tear drop

lil' diddy

I let loose
of my soul
and watched it
float into
the air
where it got stuck
in a cloud

a silken sunbeam
shot down
from the skies
and pierced the cloud
freeing my soul
and I watched it
float back
down into
me

looking

one mind
tired and burnt
scrapping the inner realms of truth
for an ounce of sanity

I'm looking into
the sleeping eyeball
waiting for answers which lie hushed
under soft warm blankets
far off in the mountains
the same mountains I climbed
in search of something
only to return home
with nothing

love

I have no diamond ring for you
I have no box of chocolates for you
the only flower I have for you
wilted during my journey back home to you

but I have a song for you
a song I sung from the top of the highest mountain
a song I sung from the depths of the darkest valley

a song I now sing to you
as you lie gentle in my arms
hushed
and warm
under our bed of stars so bright

gold over the hills

I remain with them
together as one
brothers in search of gold

we walk these hills from dawn's
breaking light
to dusk's descending darkness

never do we fail
never do we whimper

only under the foot of a passing stranger
do we struggle
do we falter

in due time we'll return to the underground
with precious gifts for our love

new

I'm new
I'm new again
I'm new into here
gone from there

I'm new in the eyes of God

I'm new in form and shape
feelings and rhyme

I'm new
I'm new again
I'm new into the sunset
gone from the sunrise

I'm new in your eyes
gone from your lies

I'm new
I'm new again
I'm new unto me
gone from thee

ramble

I'm speakin' in twisted rhymes
rememberin' them sugar coated lines
you dressed me up in
those winter nights we shivered in
come rollin' back to my mind again
where your silver spoon is a tappin'
at my glass
soon to shatter it, alas

I'm ramblin' fast
stuck in the past
like a june bug in its suburban
front yard trap

I know its been said
your mind has been fed
with worthless words clothed in lace
I'm lookin' to you for an ounce of hope
as I turn blue in the face

you send me on my way
to the break of day
to the night time sway
of the weeping willow
and I lay down my head
on a pillow of stars

we can't turn back now
we've rode too far

changing time

a snowflake fell
from the summer sky
and all was thought
inane
impure
like a sunset
never seen
a dream
never dreamt

the clock struck noon
twice within an hour
casting off all hopes
and fears
we conceived when night
met day

it is now fair to say
that once the hour glass
has emptied onto itself
it can easily be
turned over again
and again
and
again

set the sun on fire

he was born in darkness
the light that was smothered by fear
he was weaned in sadness
lamenting those he held dear

and they told him he would
catch the sun on fire
they told him to set the sun on fire
but he never could
no, he never would

he fell in love with a stranger
one cold autumn day
she placed his heart in a Gucci purse
and quickly drove away

and they told him he would
catch the sun on fire
they told him to set the sun on fire
but he never could
no, he never would

he met Death's shadow at the end of the road
with a friendly handshake and casual wink
he emptied his heavy load
they rode on together into the endless night
alone and forsaken in a weary world
void of all hope except fright

and they told him he would
catch the sun on fire
they told him to set the sun on fire
but he never could

no, he never would

riding around

it's time for me
to take you home
we've been riding around
your neighborhood for hours
silent
waiting for answers

not a single drop of noise
has broken this summer silence

I guess our end is here
there's not much we can do now

let's stop at the park
one last time for time's sake
and we'll sit on the bench
and you can hold me

tell me everything's
gonna be ok

you can kiss me on the cheek
and tell me I'll find
another someday

look to the sky
the stars are bright
yet they've been dead for years

she completes me

she gets high
from time to time
she smiles
when absurdity transpires
she walks
in rhythm with feeling
she kisses
my cheek at the strike of noon
she loves me gently
under the light of a new moon
she's my sunken treasure
lost in the Atlantic sea
she's my missing puzzle piece
she completes me

March 5 2005

it's almost midnight
and my stomach is churning
from the 2 pots of coffee and half
a pack of cigarettes I've consumed
attempting to write a piece of bullshit
that explains the way I feel about you
the way I feel about life
the way I feel

I'm out of thoughts
I'm out of feelings
I just want to go
and not stop going
until I get there

pome2423

I'm stuck
on a canvas
playing with
paint

watch me mix
night into day
with a few colors
and a blue brush
while I whistle
white words
into the rain
waiting for you
to tremble again

<u>a country song</u>

big ol' train
zoomin' down the line
ain't got no destination
Lord knows, ain't got no sense of time

big ol' train
chuggin' down the tracks
I'm headin' out baby
I won't be commin' back

I'm headin' towards that sun
settin' yonder in the sky
I ain't gettin' any younger here
and I'm fed up with yer stinkin' lies
so I'm takin' this here train
to the end of tomorrow
where, in women and whiskey
I'll gleefully wallow

someday

the autumn air has set sail
blowing dead leaves from the trees
and pushing away summer's warm touch
bringing a long since dead year back to life

we held each other closely then
we had the world and gave it away for a kiss

you taught me love
the insides and outsides of passion
you brought a dream to life

I've grown bitter since then
living in a world without you
but, sometimes when the carnival bells
and children's joyous shouts sound inside my mind
I think back to you
and feel a warmth so tender
so true
that I realize everything is ok
and we'll find each other again someday

Spring

there's birds in the trees
bees on the porch
the grass is dancing in a gentle breeze

Spring is here again!
Spring is here again!

Winter has come and gone
bringing forth heartache and pain
and taking it back again

we've got a second chance
let's not blow it this time

I'm heading overseas
where once again you'll be mine

<u>drinking beer on a coffee night</u>

I'm drinking beer
on a coffee night

I'm binge listening to the Bright Eyes
now every song sounds whiney and punk'd

I need a cigarette yet I'm too lazy to get up
so I'll sit silent and still
and dream of our most daring love endeavors
that happened so long ago
that maybe they didn't even happen at all

to Nirvana

oh, Nirvana
dame so sweet
will ya hold me
in your dreams
will ya kiss me
beneath your sheets

my dear Nirvana
how I long
for your sweet kiss
will you pat me
on the back
and tell me
I'm the one you miss

12:18

I waited on the sidelines
for a Golden opportunity
which came and passed with the speed
of a receding tide

I'm fine, really
reality has never treated us kindly
we've always wanted
what we couldn't have

Paris Blues

I'm dancing with her old ghost
down sidewalks littered with poems and piss
drunk and lost with her stealing kisses
and lines of rhymes from my heart
she's found alone by the fountain
'tis our love dressed in wilted rose petals
light me another cigarette, ma'am and
toss these joys down the metro line
and watch them emerge from the Seine clothed in bliss

oh, Mona Lisa
where were you when time stood naked upon the Sacre Coeur
o'er looking milky innocence
and Dali painted my mustache
with penile erected brush
you must have been locked in your secret case
being eye seduced by wandering tourists
who'd all love to steal that divine kiss
which tauntingly dangles from
Da Vinci's perfectly painted lips

I'm sex dried and starving
hungry for lust and midnight moons
this all time low has hit the top
and bubbled over upon your shoulder
red hot tears are burning
the cobble stone pavement in Pere-Lachaise
where the dead are dancing
dancing soft into the night
dancing into the light which beckons
the innocence of sad eyed empty stomached bums
who gracefully offer up their bread
and split pea soup for music
and a stranger's warm smile

we found these songs long ago
which carry us onward
songs proudly sung at sunset

songs which melt love into hate
pain into rain
and pure dream passion
into a nightmare fading out

where are you tonight, lone gal
bearer of my heart
at home beating the lilies
with deep blue eyes
I'm lost on the sidewalk
remembering you

I saw a city

I saw a city's blinking lights
I saw people fight over money
I saw people fight over love
they looked the same

I saw hobos eating split-pea soup with baguettes
I saw a cemetery's gates close at dusk
I saw a woman crying over a man
I saw that man get drunk and fall down

I saw lovers lusting on the banks of the river
I saw tourists looking for something to look at
I saw children with ice cream smiles
I saw a city that looks like every other city I've ever seen
the only difference was
this city saw me

to Bukowski

"no, I don't want to call you
it's too late to bother with finding the phone
and I've gotta finish this 12 pack before dawn.

no, I don't want to see you tomorrow
last I've heard, you've gained some weight and have
become a bigger bitch than you were with me
anyways, I've got a date with Jessica tomorrow night."

she signs offline without another word

I take a sip of my now warm beer
finish a line to poem that I've been working on all night
and crawl into bed with Kelly

one last time

you had it all planned out
from day one
you knew the ending outcome
as I sat and watched it
all unfold

you cut me not once
but twice
leaving me on the sidelines to bleed these
feelings dry

somehow I survived

there's no doubt
I'm living on borrowed time
with a failing liver
and sutured heart

I hear the church bells chime
as I kiss your cold hand
one last time

<u>7:50</u>

hours are in negative space
and I'm floating in broken lines
and you're waxing the clock's
second hand with your
filthy rag
and we're not looking to the sky anymore
the sun has burned our eyes
but the light in our hearts continue to flicker
and memories fuel this dying flame

a.m longings

good times are
a pierced eye-brow
and burning hair
precisely placed
upon a face
of grandeur and beauty
so sweet
so well known to many
in other shapes
but this form
I hold dear

you called my name
from a far
and I dreamt of a billion
nights by your side

<u>one is 4</u>

looking up
up to the sky
my eyes wander
in the blue ebbed stillness
as I stumble upon
a golden ray of hope

I'm dancing with
a diamond disaster
in a heavy afternoon haze
of children's dope

SHot

I tried watching
as you pierced the moon
with a spinning wheel
but my mind was distracted
by children weeping
at a falling star

I tried watching
as you moved like a thunderstorm
over a desperate land
but my heart fell to the ground
and I had to bend down
to pick it back up

I tried watching
as you attempted to piece
together an infinite pieced puzzle
but I got bored and went home

I tried watching you
with my pink eye
but realized you were
a waste of time

sound

a dry well
situated deep down

falling in and out of
consciousness

is a song a song
without sound?

subsiding anxiety

my temper is complete
with calm nerves
and empty lungs

the mid-afternoon sunshine
chimes thru the window
melting away this icy emptiness

there's chopped wood sitting
in piles in the back of
my neighbor's yard

summer is on her way

where are we going

where have they all gone
my friends from the past
what are they spending their lives on nowadays
where am I going with this empty suitcase
blank notepads and bountiful books
where have you gone with your pencils and pens
brushes and endless canvases

I don't know
and I don't care to know

I'm really only worried about us
and what we're doing
and where we're going
and if we're worthy of this feast on the table
and if we deserve to drink this wine before us
and if we even deserve anything at all

we substituted karma for Cadillacs long ago

on a dream

these streets are never too dead for dreaming
there's always an ounce of memory
that drags behind along the sidewalk
of the past
and it always catches up to you
when you're least expecting it
reminding you of once was
reminding you of what can be
some things end up lost
and there ain't much you can do
but hope it finds a good home
elsewhere

nature's knives

hell is abstract
thoughts at the dawn
of the day

gold hues laced with
black blues

wishful thoughts on
a fleeting summer morning
perform their red-eye'd magic
in another suburban front yard

car engines start
humming
then roll off into the horizon
where nothing is known
where there is so much
to be learned
where there is so much
to be forgotten

dew damp kisses
are conceived in fall
and run dry by the
same time next year

it's only nature
performing with her knives
over our humble heads

I know it's right

listen to the silent cries
of a distant charade

they're still and smooth
like an early morning hangover
coated in honey

bed sheets are wrinkled
clothes on the floor
what is all this emotion good for
hand me my shoes and a parting kiss
and I'll find the door

all of this unknowingness has become too familiar
I'm too content in the face of change
I tremble not when confronted by danger
I only cry at the notion of a stale goodbye

I'm going to the store
where I'll be sure
to pick up your cigarettes
and a TV Guide

I believe in this land

tick-tocking time
down to despair

I felt a cool creation
upon my brow
as I sought a distant land

hovering above congealed waves
swaying in stopped motion
conversing with gods
dancing with angels

I only call home
home if I can freely
hang my hat upon
the wall

I believe the streets
are paved with gold
not the glittering kind
that is searched out for in malls
or boutiques
but the kind that shimmers
in the soul of animate beings

I believe that people
are saints in disguise
composing immaculate poems
in their minds
as they waltz these golden streets
from sunset
to sunrise

I believe in this land
as it is meant to be believed in
it undresses fear for you
and leaves her standing nude
in your presence

when my feet touch the ground
reality will be replaced
by phantasy
and a ghost will be born

I need new

I can't stand the thought of
continuing like this
living like a worn out memory
in a place I use to call home

I need new places

I need new people

I need
New

NEw

NEW

out with the old!

my heart has run out of feelings
my tear ducts are dry
but my soul is stronger than ever
or I'm just less sensitive

either way
I'm bending my last
sun ray
attempting to squeeze out
this last drop of inspiration

no one

no one can see the tears
streaming down from her bloodshot eyes
as she gives her last kiss
to her first love

no one can feel the pain
that stabs her side
as she enters her father's car
and rides into the stormy sunrise

there's a small fractured dream
dangling from a rain cloud
and a poem I wrote on a napkin
that lies wrinkled and torn
on the pavement

one more dance

you said that it's
time for you to go
that you have nothing
left to show

I've read your words
over and over
you've wiped my tears
like a humble lover

but before you leave
let's have one more dance

one more dance
under the street's neon lights
one more dance
in the middle of this sultry summer night
one more dance
to a tune I don't know
one more dance
love me
let me go

remembrance in a future age

my stomach is empty
void of hunger

yet my heart is content
full of little longings

my hands are bare
minus the cigarette that is
caught between my middle and index
fingers which is attempting to finger
an instant thought that pops
into my mind like internet spyware

I just end up clicking it away
and its lost forever

all I have left is a broken book
from an unknown author who lived a woeful life
and died a depressing death

I'm heading down his same path
with a notebook, pen and a black slouch cap draped over my head

klicks and pops

lightly tapping

drum patting

klicks
&
pops

t
w
i
s
t
s

and easy turns

an echo poised
on a rainbow-ridden canvas

slowly crashing piano riffs glide

d
o
w
n

and collide
upon a smile

severed
and sincere

ghosts

an urn poised on the edge of a hill
bearing month old plastic flowers
which have faded a bit with the passing days

the dirt is still fresh
the straw lies sparse
an ant rummages through the grass which
has begun growing around your headstone
the plaque which bears your name
sparkles in my eyes under the light
of a mid-noon summer sun

Grandpa's plate has become worn and
tarnished over the years
I never knew him
never heard the stories he would tell
or the hugs he would've shared
never knew what a great guy he was

but I knew you
dear Grandmother
I knew you and your love
your love that never ran low
your love that stretched the miles
and always found me whether I was near or far
your love that I thought had left me when you did

yet as I stand next to you and Grandpa now
I sense it within me
the love I never knew
and the love I'll never forget

I feel it now more than ever

words

words
words
words

they're all I have to
describe what I'm feeling

no touches
nor kisses
no fist fights
or kicks
just a simple arrangement of the alphabet
can sum up what I'm thinking
what I've felt
and what I'll feel

life's not fair
nothing's fair
except the spinning of the Ferris wheel
at the local county fair
where ya can be with the stars for
a moment in time
where ya can look down over the
town you've called home for too long
and think over a life you've denied
defining over again

Paris Scribblings (July 2005)

Places des Vosges

sitting in Places des Vosges
watching and waiting for
one more glimpse into the
eyes of bliss

———————————

gray skies look particularly
lovely as they float
past Parisian rooftops

———————————

pitter-patter
waterfalls wait
for the click of a camera
tourists chuckle
the rain begins falling
and the tourists sadly
waltz back to their
$20.00 rooms

———————————

moving right along
with little money
and pounds of thoughts
that must find their
way to this paper

———————————

let's dress up this
revolution in a tuxedo
and hand it a glass of wine

it'll make these streets
of blood shine

_____

Gare du Nord

easy they come
even easier they go
people in search
of that light
which so brightly
burns within

_____

Quai d'Anjou

the skies have turned
from light blue
to pale gray
the rivers are green
and full of debris
cars pass with an unclear
destination
bums lie content
in warm blankets beside
the quai
and I'm nursing a poem
where Morrison and Baudelaire
once nursed theirs

far away

a new moment unfolds
a new touch of time
a girl so sweet and carefree
oh, how her smile shines
her kisses so soft and delicate
and a heart that beats long and true
her words stretch the miles
hitting me when I need them the most
I'm counting down the days until we meet again
arms and eyes intricately intertwined
with a mouth full of stories to share

<u>silent sighs</u>

Saint Antoine misses our late night tender kisses we tossed each other in front of Jim
Morrison's last quiet apartment

Rue De La Roquette misses your desperate shouts in search of your friend who was actually
farther away than we anticipated but safe nonetheless

Gare Du Nord recalls the time when we thought you were leaving and wept a tear after a
warm parting embrace only to find out you were in the wrong train station and another day
was ours to share

and how can the Seine forget that day when we sat nervous and sober gazing off into the
distance anticipating our impending end
as strangers ate their bread and wine and tourists snapped photographs alongside us

it was all just a moment of honey dripping from a silly moon

fairy book romance

I'm forming a moment of bliss on my eyelids
heavy sensations shake me down
a wishful descent into the unknown
a look of despair

bleak castles and sparkling rainbows hide in the shadows
catacombs of lost writings
from poets I've never known
run deep underground
starlit moonbeams fall to the floor
illuminating a silver second
in which time melts
and every bad thought is erased
cast into the unknown

and all that's left is you
standing like a fair maiden
in a fairy book romance
hair in the wind
eyes to the sky

<u>keep it to yourself</u>

keep it to yourself
your ghostly secrets of a gothic romance
keep it to yourself
the shadows that play inside your mind
I'm due for a physical soon
and my soul's in shackles

dig these old words
dig THIS old word of THAT bard
ancient and tender
fresh and gay
take it for granted
or live by it
your moves are yours
and yours alone, my love

just keep it to yourself

spoon-feeding happiness

do you hear the rain outside of your window

do you care if you get wet

can you smile off a grudge

that was placed on your heart

when you were with me long ago

touchy turns around broken road corners

occupy my mind

riverboat dreams floating downstream

occupies yours

are you safe indoors tonight

does your head feel alright

as you pop your last three pills

and look to your mirror

brilliant beauty

blind eyes
behind a beat

smoke ridden voices
chime as bodies
sway in rhythm to
the pulse of
a spitting record

bip-bop
tippity-top

lights flicker
in
and
out

I watch her
from the side

a brilliant beauty
bathed in sound

being alive

I remember those autumn days
when it all seemed appropriate
learning and living were separated into equal amounts
my heart spread its wings to love
and life continued with reason as it has and always will

you were my halo
and I your faithful servant
ready and willing to open up to anything you presented unto me
there were no mystical visions or holy longings
no fear, no emptiness
I felt well as I sang songs
and drank the finest wines
with you alongside me

that day when we sat swinging softly on your summer hammock
I saw a bird perched high on a twig
with a special gleam in its eye
I saw the blades of grass dance fervishly in the breeze
of a cascading day
I saw the feather of desire and every touch of sin
melt into the blazing sun

it was all life
it was the joys of being alive
and feeling real

enlightenment

my soul awaits for the inevitable
I wonder what life holds in store for us

the ocean tide rolls in then out
bringing in the new
whilst removing the old

maybe that's what we are
waves soon to be washed away by other waves
and in turn, finding our meaning
out at sea

I play on this song
a disaster of dreams
a hodgepodge of reality

take me in for face value
as there's nothing inside
but an empty cage slowly corroding

music has the answers for the questions we ask

there's a knock at my door
Fate stands silently waiting like a nervous whore brought upstairs
I let her in and offer her a beer
after a few hours of shy sighs
she opens for me
an orgasmic truth of self ponderings are revealed
and in an instant she is gone
yet I remain with a head full of aches
and a shaft full of pearly white wisdom

<u>ramble reprise</u>

sea-monster bleeding blue
I've seen it once
'twas you I thought I knew
bed blankets covered in sleep
dreams lie awake
weary w/ fatigued creep

the ashes which lie sprinkled on the sullen floor
are a result of a demonic catastrophe
brought forth by an old maid of a witch
she breeds spells in NY and casts matured
hexes onto the minds of willing gentlemen
-a golden abortion transpires
silvery seconds slip by as the heart continues pulsating
until it slows...softens
& its sound is silenced

with your silk eyes you catch me
with your fair words you own me
with your sweet love you slay me
forever I can rest
in your gentle garden
all eternity is spread out before me
now and now only can I see
the real you

tempting the unattainable

rain clouds gather around me
as I wait for her to speak

riddles of broken chords
and a heavenly hangover of
blue pills describe me
in stars uncharted

the window blinds are open
and life plays its game outside

swimming through a migration
of summer birds
I search for you
only to find you ahead of the pack

yes you, Winter's angel dressed in white
and me, Summer's devil clothed in purple

behind you I glide
always attempting to catch up
always attempting for the unattainable

I thought you

I thought you
a purpose to reason
a black season
a treason of the heart

you gave me a disease
in the mind

crazy thoughts occupy me
deny me
to a real truth

I've searched my way out
only to find you
looking into
a broken mirror

a blank canvas that will soon be the sad holder of a wonderful painting

my fate
held softly in your hands
you watch the world move
in and out
you forgot what you meant
to remember
or you forgot what you meant
to forget
I blame the sunset
it can change a thought
into a dream
it can change a feeling
into a tear

to the madcap (madcap melodies)

-   Syd Barrett

does my mind click
to your match in a
proper manner
do you fall at first glimpse
of goddess voice strumming
near your ear

the flowers in the garden lay dead
behead by an instant of self-doubt

no more seaside waves
no more inlaid paths to follow
the woods are heavy with fog
and you gave up trying to find your
way out long ago

only a simple nude canvas
and tubes of acrylics arouse you
to chance

life is but a chance
sometimes you make it
sometimes you make it and fall
sometimes you never make it at all

coincidently Paris

a day café
breaks the gray of an
afternoon rain
sitting at a small table with an
espresso and cigarette
flicking ashes onto the sidewalk
as people walk by

turn on your heart

when your friends are gone
and no one can turn a helpin' hand
when your land's all dried up
like long lost desert sand
and all the water in the whole wide world
won't help
and all the smilin' faces are quick to melt
you can find an ounce of hope
when you turn on your heart
and refuse to mope or pout
after all this is what life is all about
hard time's come
stay a bit then go
and you're left with golden experience
which you can proudly show
you'll be picked out in a crowd of fifteen hundred
as the person who stood tall
never stumbled or plundered
so when the days done and gone
and everything around you
looks false and wrong
just listen to that ol' heart a-thumpin' in your chest
it'll cast out all the bad
and leave you with the best

move 4th

beside the river does it grow
a rose of eternal joy
each petal so finely scented
each thorn so perfectly pointed
oh, how every passer-by wishes to posses
such a marvel of creation

I dare you to move forth
and bring unto this humble emptiness
a gift so sincere, so righteous
as to make the angels of love tremble
beneath their sea of stars

I await your answer

365 days of silence grows stronger
by the moment
with every passing breath I breathe
with every word that slips from my tongue
with every thought which is born in my mind

my desire to see you clothed in moonlight
dancing as a wild springtime lily would
in a long since barren field
arouses itself to notorious delicacy

see this through

the season's in transition
reasons are too heavy to carry
and these breathing memories
can't be buried

for you I'm sure it's true
that heaven looks red
and hell seems blue
I've seen it through and through
to wait around would suffice things twice
once for me
and once for you

only if you move
only if you set into the groove which chimes by your ear
only if you can hear me calling to you

let's see this through

a girl (that falls like the rain)

there's a new voice in my room tonight
assuring me that everything's gonna be alright
and with the flick of a switch she whispers my name
oh, how I love a girl that falls like the rain

my friends wonder why I live so fast
putting the future behind me along with the past
I can only smile and remind them that nothing good will last
and flirt with a new love who'll take me home tonight
they're all the same
oh, how I love a girl that falls like the rain

they all try their best to replace her with many tricks
some try longer than others but they just ain't as slick
as she was when she left me with a heart full of bricks
they always end up thinking its no use, I'm insane
but oh, how I love a girl that falls like the rain

on a card

dear dove
flying high
what rhymes can you
share for her and I

poems of passion
inspiration everlasting
messages sent across the sky

dear dove
flying high
what rhymes can you
share for her and I

a shake at noon

she gave it all away
as she sang her reasons
to those willing to listen

cigarette ashes
left gathered in an ashtray
were scattered by her voice
as she gave it all away
her purpose for seasons
to those willing to listen

a soft abstraction
painted painfully onto
a canvas
saw her give it away
her truce to her being
to all of them people
willing to listen

and below this
morning breeze
a church organ
punctuated her voice
giving it all away
to everyone willing to listen

watching this worries me

a photograph links a thought to the mind
and brings it to the surface when ready
to shed itself of its old skin

these little catastrophes
light flashes of
headaches and clapping chills
tidy up a dirty day

could you please remember
to forget

watching this worries me

the only thing that seems to be real
is on vacation
and its far too smooth to be
found out

yes, I admit
watching this worries me

our love is all we have
our love is worth more than any jewel
or piece of land
our love is all we have
and all we need

when you return

have you found
the spinning sound
to set your soul in motion

are you wishing for that
mystical awakening in
a nude idea

does a natural surrounding
drive you home

II

a diamond disaster

hello again

I give myself another chance

opening inwards to find

what was once thought lost

shadows of old ghosts greet me

& wish me all the best

I begin again

moving with ease

along this all too

familiar highway

sweet galaxy

you have a sweet galaxy
a comfortable pain to numb
a heartless rhyme

your time extends far
far off into the distance
straight to my door

quiet nights spent
listening to messages from
you, feeling a real feel swim
thru these veins

no more pain

no more pain
I loosen myself to it
& feel no more

camera flashes
& heavy-caked eyelashes
find me Saturday night
with a sincere
simplistic perspective
drowned out

with a whimsical melody
found on your belly-ring

I dance

no more pain
I loosen myself to it
& feel no more

sounds of a falling sky

this transportation is too tacky

must we travel this quickly to our

destinations

I'd rather sail silently in a ship

lost at sea

yeah, that's where I'd rather be

simply wishing the best

simply wishing the best

as memories are born into themselves once more

I can see from my bedroom window

a waiting stranger ready to make a move

I dedicate this poem to delight

sentimental sculptures in my head,

fire in the stomach,

a live as to be living

& not what thought once was

oh, oh, oh

I sing you

in all melodies as sweet

as a piece of pastel

sliding slowly across a

blank page

mystery mountains of Mexico

mystery mountains of flames

catching mystics in a kiss

you lie awake during night

counting the stars

looking out far for something more

a spinning moment leaves you

wanting something

we'll never find

hell after office hours

what we've seen
is enough to string us
along for another moment or 2

our fears delay
as we wait

our heart's beat out a melody
of stock markets and deadlines

the paper is pink on the desk
pen is black
words mean less than what
the mind conceives
as they are written with nervous ease

a trip to hell
chrome caves and metallic
fire-lined displays

a sweet voice strums next to your ear
requesting your company on a
compelling adventure

with no hesitation
you follow

walkin'

I go to your window
but the blinds have been pulled down
I call your house
and your sister says you ain't around
I go to the places where we use to go
and I never find you there
oh, you must be with a new man
and Lord, that ain't no fair

well, the winter winds blow so uneasy
out here on the open road
I just have to keep a-walkin'
I may never rest this heavy load
but I know you'll be warm tonight
in the arms of that new man

I'll keep a-walkin'
from east to west clear 'cross
this fair land
yea, I'll keep a-walkin'
'til this burden ain't so heavy
I'll keep a-walkin'
'til I find someone true to marry

11/24/2005

Thanksgiving day on a limb

keeping inside what should remain unborn

odd 30 second phone calls which seem

like an eternity

a welcomed break from this self-imposed

reality which I find myself staggering around in

the handshakes are dry and insincere

and vanish as quickly as they are produced

if I could explain what you are a little better

I could hold onto all of this with a much firmer grip

far from home

do you miss your family and friends
who always gave you that helping hand in
your times of need

do you miss me waking up by your side
and those strawberry kisses we shared
oh, so sweet

sweet memories seem so bitter
when you're all alone
so far, far from home

what do you think of when
evening rolls around in all of her mystery

are you scared and cold
or do you feel safe in the arms of another
are his kisses as sweet as mine

sweet memories seem so bitter
when you're on your own
so far, far from home

lemon haunted sighs

can I bend her soul the right way

as to allow a little more space into mine

how long can she wait in this superficial surrounding

without appearing vague with lemon haunted sighs

I push through all of this and find nothing

nothing to allude these cravings for simpler times

nothing to dismay the unbreakable tongues of the natives

I've lost myself again

as I curl up in my sheets and fall asleep

with her love again

all of these agains must end and let IT begin

butterflies

slowly getting drunk

falling back into the past

where life seems so real

every word is catching up to me

your breath has grown bitter

I love it nonetheless

purple-winged butterflies float

past these scenes

with distant skies full of rain

and this pain which I try to hide

my soul seeks a wanting

which waits down the road

in all of its tenderness sublime

searching for a smile in a supermarket

longing to take you home

and teach you what I've yet to learn

salvation for a tear stained book

face to face

a force inside a dream

contemplating galaxies being born

& unborn in unison

falling stars cover our fear

smoking my last cigarette with simple pleasure

I missed our last opportunity to heaven

God knows best

as I sit here now pondering what He ponders

did you tremble in the trees

shadows of heart breaks

deliver my mail to a new address

I won't be in this town much longer

the rolling seas call me

clear skies with blotches of clouds

paint me this way

I saw you through the glass and smiled

salvation for a tear stained book

you read when all was dead

what is alive now

tomorrow's morning

simplicity knows not of our adventures
or wars we fought under the moonlit fields
where blood ran wild
through the misty grass

evolution was drunk and made love
to the saint of disguise
& bore infinite children of corruption & rust

my soul is free to carry this movie on
with no clear plot
only a bitter climax which will stir your tears to the top

remember the mountain and leaves
the wind through your dress
the brown of the mud on your knees
remember me for now
for the light of nuclear suns will chime in tomorrow's
morning & who knows where we'll be

managing a machine

lost in the midst of a day dressed in shine
& glow

what's more for this surgery
everything you worked for came out
as much less

a steady patter of dangling
drops of water caught on a faucet head
your every wish lies rotting and dead
in your head
we pry it open with pens and rulers
and chart its contents on a worn notepad
this feels so bad
yet it satisfies the beast within

I saw you leaving
wearing nothing but black
you left your soul on the counter
& forgot to come back

beneath a lime light

wishing on a dime

break me outta this line
of empty bedrooms &
wrinkled sunsets

a notion pales at the mere
mention of a feeling

I apologize for disturbing
your lack of interest
& replacing your face with hers

maybe we can carry this
self-mutilation over to the
next room where the light limes
after a minute of dealing out all of
these tricks

are you sick of me yet?

letting go of forever

with this one form
holding the distance
a static sun sets
on the horizon

when you shake off
this momentum
& see the world from
your window

when you become
what you fear
& let go of
forever

for forever is not
long enough
here

well worn wishes

one circle
painted green
the path to heaven
lit by darkness
the true heart
sees nothing
but love
yet our fears
push it away

a vast array
of dismal hues
swim under the moon's
fertile umbra

I decipher the meaning
of this moment
and it sneaks into
my soul
in the form of
a dream

countless delusions
infused inside complex
creations

your eyes follow me
from this dream
to the next

honest atmosphere

- S.K

subtle sincerities
imitate fingers
collapsing with mouths
full of letters

I see you in a pool
of dilated colours

your rhythm
a web of surprise
piano riffs dictate time
as violins dissect the perimeter
where you wait for me
to sit with you
and lose our hearts
to a honest atmosphere

sepia-toned lies

beer stains
on my wooden desk
how many beers
will it take
to erase an unwanted
memory

with the panicked cry from unforgetful friends
on the prowl for uncured desires
blessed with a tune explaining
half of what im feeling

I see her in a new picture
with another man
and I'm feeling numb
dumb of me to have felt any different before
as these emotions
often make for a bore
of a tale

questions go unanswered
literature crucified for lust
words rust
under this new rain-filled spring-time morning
when even the sun is too lazy to rise

I gaze into her sepia-toned eyes
to find a face full of lies
so cute, so deadly
that I'm left feeling so badly

trading in this old heart
for a new one
I die again
and with a brush to her chin
she readily welcomes it

brush strokes: a dance

impressionism on stage
swimming in satin lights
and an easy smile
God chimes in thru
the bass line
leaving her liberated

no dollar can
crucify this song
no whisper is worth
a kiss

her skirt falls to the floor

I want nothing more
than this

every move sketched from
pure ideas
nothing over-the-top

this dance
a puzzle
with a million little perfect
pieces I place together
with an intuitive inspiration

she owns me with a few
crumbled dollars

upon waking

catching the sun
in first eyes upon waking
shaking off dreams for
what they are
a delayed coffee brew
grasping pill with water
and brushing teeth
all tuned to a silent speaker
producing sinister songs

phone rings
voicemail left
what is there to be said
that cannot be said
thru this spring silence

new spring

children walking down
swollen streets
with bicycles and trampolines
squirrels shagging
barking dogs
and mowing grass
a dead mosquito on my
nephew's new floor
falling earlier
and rising with the sun
sequenced with vivid
television dreams
odd nights moving
in the music
over whiskey and coke
where her eyes
meet mine
with my restful receipt
holding her phone number

what's in an age

judging by this creative whim
caught on your turquoise jacket
you've collected pieces like this before

swimming in incandescent, sick lights
we meet with smiles
& mental handshakes
a cool way to finish the day
or start it
depending upon which side of the glass
one's eyes peer through

voices never connected
the broken bookshop phone booth
would never allow it
yet they do now
under the light of seduction
and theft

what is left of love
this word does nothing for me anymore
even you, sweet beholder of my modern heart
cannot slay me
cannot move me like in days of old
when I would not sleep for nights
thinking of beauty exposed

writing now
with you in mind
I remain indifferent

twice removed

prophetic songs
at appropriate times

transforming a picture
into reality
and back into
a day dream

silence juxtaposed
by seemingly endless
wires and waves

star struck lust

captivators gather around
the seconds waiting
for a simple whimper
a tear to fall
a breath to breathe
an Armageddon to arrive
like an arrow to the chest
like a ravening guitar lost
playing on a horizon

and in this gin and tonic
I find the answers
once removed from your breast
twice removed from your
heart

a coming summer

keeping up with modern
words, poems and prose
aisles full of books
with the sparse book attendant looking
fine in her tight pants
in her I see Neal Cassady swooning over
a girl in a restaurant
or Hemingway drooling over bulls
and wine of Spain

Rimbaud lost in Africa

she wants me to meet her in New York
teach her what she doesn't know
and maybe gain a kiss outta the whole scene
yet my passion lies in the disco bars
full of gin and bubble gum pop

and the streets
with their endless lessons

I'll hail a taxi
and regret it all
by morning

either way

delays in cinematic landscapes
riding, unaware, into a night full of
clouds, stars, music and gum
our destination lies on the outskirts
of a never ending circle
sending us in search of something
that cannot be found

parents, blood protectors
of their young ones
willing to spend what's earned
to be sanctified in safety

on the front porch
peering out upon the lawn
glass of water and unease

its a mystery
an answer we'll find over time
time being the enemy
the days pass like poison
to the veins

it could go either way

Satan at the right time

breaking out the morning tunes
shaking out the devil
with dew drops & coffee

voices in the middle
chant in unison
like a leering chorus

telephone talk in 2 ways
a misplaced translation
a new feeling for
this midweek

I love you more
when I die like this

bleeding poetry

I lie on my bed
bleeding poetry

imagery floods the floor

what more is to be asked for

thoughts come as a feather
and words are quick to dissolve
I mend frayed songs with wrinkled literature
and expect innocence to be portrayed perfectly

I ask for it all

bleeding this poetry
leaves me heaving like a fiend
without junk

I tremble
waiting for it

action figures
and comic books
easier times are getting sicker

all I'm left with is this cancer called maturity
my redemption lies in pens
and paper dabbled in rhymes

the winter cold outside
meeting the hum of a warm
radiator captures me

a loving bullet

blending emotions in with rain
capturing a moment with a kiss
that I can taste throughout the day
words breaking at the speed of light

what soul is without fright
and fear for the unknown

moving too fast
or not fast enough
moving with ease
like a gentle breeze
blowing through newly sculpted hair

no one ever told you it would be fair

all of these little inklings in the heart
like a bullet leaving the barrel of a loving gun
slowly finding its victim on the
outskirts of daydream

holding your scent

they've got knives
buried in their hearts
and a boiling blood falling
down, burning the floor

I've stole your diamonds
and drank your wine
I'm making out like a priest
with a head full of jilted prayers
yet I'm killing myself with flowers
and bones

and you're wishing for a ring to
sing you into the future
no allusions to then
I've erased it with your wine
and found it again while cleaning
up the pieces of your life

my hands still hold your scent
after a day's worth of work

sun

sun, no picture inside...burning it all fucking down
sun where it all happens..and happens again and again and again
sun-fire like the moon is cold or blue..replacing everything with nothing
and nothing with the Sun who burns me inside out
where I become one with the Sun again
I'm borne into the Sun, a son I am
pauper to silly phate...missing Sun once more
all relative philosophies are nulled without the Sun's ever potent presence
sun burns Van Gogh's acrylics in half a second
and gives me this light to write by
so said I to the Sun
that one day I will die and forever run
alongside you

what speak of this (car crash at midnight)

relapsing after recovery
tree tales of broken car crashes
shedding a tear in a strip club
baby cribs endorsed by empty
bottles of beer
dry glasses of wine
and a sleepy cry for my love

what speak of this

dozing off in anger
captured nonchalantly
in a prophetic painting
purple slit into a fading blue-red
yellow lines- organic

dew songs at dusk

the parade is now over
and everyone has left to go home
returning new-phound knowledge
into weeping machinery
products of helplessness
and decay

goodbye

-MB

meeting you once more

over a handshake and hug

drunken promises

a dry tear

a leash to hold back reality

living in time so real

funeral home chanting

bagpipes on national anthem

you arrive late

green telephone rings

redemption in coffee

cigarettes

and losing lottery tickets

a goodbye

edge of death

on the edge of death

trees scarred

brutal beatings of the brain

love lost on a tragic hwy

test of time

mother losing son

brother losing brother

friend losing friend

can the test of time

stand now

gates

the gates close in an hour

60 minutes left to work our art
over on them

skies sick with smoke
an occasional star peeping thru

treadless tires
tackle thin streets

empty reflections
in occupied mirrors

the Lords gather
breaking the alphabet while
mending strophes

all alone
with Muslim eyes

lost at sunset

cutting the coast
with bare feet
alone, wasting the sunset

the king and queen's nervous eyes
rattle our fragile foundation

a dog, lost, finding its way thru
this twisted labyrinth
where i lost myself a long time ago

shadows at evening tide gather
ghost dance on waves
a dark roar of ocean air...

mistaking confusion (cotton candy and fireworks)

mistaking this confusion
by a simple illusion of you
against a back-drop of Ferris wheels
and cotton candy

seeing the sun set
and night arrive in her washed-out glow
sprinkled with fireworks erupting

say this ain't so

bluez for Dublin

there's no way out

each moment leads to this

washed up in the same old place

looking for a new face to

show the way

who's to say

that its supposed to be like this

setting my alarm clock for morning

I wait

math in g minor

he's selling penny passports over the border
she's cleaning the kitchen for her guests
Johnny Rotten was seen weeping for order
and I got green growing from my chest

all and all the post man is content
he built a new mailbox from stamps
into which he could easily vent
the Queen was killed by a confused ant
that thought she was Bin Laden
Mr. Rogers was spotted at a pub
looking a bit low and down-trodden

the disease and conceit of a foreign land
is eating away at my textbook
I'm gonna learn how to play guitar and start a band
make a lotta money, make out like a crook

forgotten hearts

filing the past into the present
bringing forth forgotten hearts
and killing off new ones

shall I watch my death with virgin eyes

pushed to the side
forgotten to a new guy
who claimed this bride
with cheap and sick bribes

killing off these seconds with alcohol

walking once more down the hall
with an angel crowned with a crooked halo
she saw it all come, go and materialize
into rushed fame

my flame has burned too long
my song is ending

everything is all but gone

Paddington

- dedicated to the victims of the July 7, 2005
terrorist attacks in London

hitting the open streets with a new taste
for what's important

casualties in the underground

internet cafes
and pints of beer

quiet seconds spent meditating in a taxi
to Camden

she meets me on the sidewalk
with a tear and welcoming embrace

I'm all alone
so far from home
searching for life
in the face of death

I'm here, you're there

will it make things easier
if I change myself for fate's sake

lone night car drives inside dark streets
midnight nightmares of death and trees
a quiet scream and soft explosion

I'm better when I'm not myself
a lover with no desires
a dreamer without dreams
a sound playing in a room without ears

I've come to see the crucifixion
I've brought rosaries and a pencil
to jot down what I most fear

nothing is near when you're here
and I'm there

beginning

dark moon over raging waters
a gold halo lit on the horizon
giving the unborne a ghastly glow

birth

ear-piercing chaotic sound
blood, fear, mystery

all creatures set in place
in one instant, all content, all well

dirt blows around and around
with the fury of 10,000 hurricanes
lightning falls upon every inch of ground

the form of man appears

witness to the past
gold chambers dissolve
a symphonic tune plays someplace
behind the sun

dissolving (in a mystery)

I'm never quite content
in this blazing star around me
I never see the love
hiding within an oak tree
I will never control inertia
thus setting the letters free

its calmly cooling down
dissolving in a mystery

what have you left
a kiss to tide my unease
what have you given
a lone, parted breeze
what of this is remaining
I beg you, tell me please

its calmly cooling down
dissolving in a mystery

east of Eden

turmoil within a family

herding sheep in til dusk

growing a forbidden fruit

an inappropriate communication

causes blood to be shed

upon strong soil

with a bag of clothes

and a heavy burden

I head off towards the

east of Eden

untitled

she smiled and showed me a star

her sullen stone of mar

her laughing willow in woods a far

I came down for a while to talk

scarecrow dancing in corn-stalk

I drew her a picture of her soul with chalk

would you be so kind as to help

would you melt my icy cloak of felt

and show me everything I can't see

untitled #2

lost in fields of mandarin and sage
opium signals flash a frightful maze
of Cadillac distress, Victorian days

in which ways have they came
look into my eyes
an image all the same
all waiting in coffee tongue

she came around for a day
painted a portrait and was on her way
to her unknown home at the edge
of Rome

brandished her smile on my arm
never meant any harm
or not much harm

untitled #3

smiling light of child's balloon
meets me in matrimony on the moon
the paling pan, sordid spoon
rusted knife, winter in June

not far off course
high on your prized Pulitzer horse
you ride into the milky way
oh, its quite a beautiful day
to see you again
its almost lovely hearing
you speak in sonnets again

seeing your gold skin bronze
beside a sandy beach
I lay beneath a calm down tree
thinking of you
eating a peach

untitled #4

she was hip as a scent
womanly flower blossoming
into abstraction
her laughs folded
her lips broke satisfaction

through the misty view
her will was viewed
in bad taste
yet her face showed
innocence

yellowing letters

there's some sweet nectar
spoken of to cure
the thirst of a
poet's tongue

I've yet to find it

searching far and close
beneath cathedral steps
inside gas station restrooms
always coming out empty hearted

though I can stare at my memories
and find a void that needs to be filled
and supplement it with cracked
photographs and yellowing letters

sometimes something

sometimes you just fade
into that misty realm
of unforgiveness and gloom
just disappear into the abyss
with pennies and pills
drowning in past lives, loves
and never look back

sometimes you burn so bright
that it blinds your eyes for
the rest of your life
only seeing what can be found
by your heart
never knowing whom the odds favor
carrying on without remorse renders
every move hopeless

sometimes you blanket distress
in sleepy hues, melt a canvas
with tears and drown yourself
in imaginary beers
or wish-wash wake into a
new dawn finding yourself
in an old bed next to a new
boy instead

baiser beauty

starlight dances upon
pernod pleasantries
wonderful scenes playing
out time and time again

her lips smooth against mine
diddling with limbs below the table
holds this conversation long and stable
'til we take it to the street

art meets the heart
baiser beauty

garments strip dark
in absent lighted room
this moment of madness
works its way in, silly
subtle and soon

a sullen stream of sonnets
floods the bed
she's got me reeling
kneeling and red

nothing I've read could ever match this
a baiser beauty
and a soft tender kiss

river walk

sit silent
listen to the hum
of this heartbeat
find the melody in your soul

sing along

oh, just another sad heart song
to move us along

gold in your cheeks
burning passion with
river walk whispers

summer lays down its heart
and with empty hands
embraces autumn's decay

what can I do

what can I say

tree branches waving
calloused stars lost in
evening's night

a lullaby of tulips
raven's flight

American Queen

American Queen
secret seducer on the sly
cracking me to pieces
with a hawk's eye

her pillbox prayers pursue me
her lighthouse leers lure me
her midnight mind murders me

beforeyaknowit we've
torn our worlds to thunder
all for the name of
newphoundwonder

crushed cupid

oh, what sweet splendour
caught in your vile smile
revolting against your very birth
which was advertised upon every
brown, wrinkled newspaper in
days of old, days of gold
days when love could not be sold

the creature still lives within you
setting you apart from others
who wish they could be you
wish they could carry beauty like you
or slay every man's frail heart like you

only you
who longs for this creature's demise
could but shortly roam these
streets scantly disguised
until some crushed cupid would
fall by you side and mutter some
sad last words and close its eyes
and die

impressions along the Seine

he's just another washed-up poet drinking sugarless coffee to clean the morning monotony. I've seen sexier angels on rue Saint Antoine fiddling around their coat pockets in search of a nickel for the port-o-potty, even more poetic when they realize, yet again, that they were broke, thus having to free themselves on the steps of the opera house.

 its a good feeling when the bars close and you find yourself drinking a dollar bottle of tokay, murdering the Seine in dumbfounded chaos. all the pretty girls are locked up in their doll tenements dreaming of the boys who will sweep them away upon white horses and head clear for the sunset, when, in all actuality, the boys have taken their bikes down into happening soirées along the riverbank and loose themselves to cheap women after succumbing to various drinks.
yes, its a nice feeling, all of this. me, spectator of the holy land, unnamed seer of this surrounding. My friends and I get lost along the Seine and end up in a forest of towers...closed business districts which breathe like a ravening monster who must breathe like this whilst lost in deep sleep...we are careful not to wake this powerful creature, though nothing but the breaking of a dollar could nudge a beast such as this in sleep.

ambitions

everyone is always asking,
"what is your life's ambition?"
and say this, knowing you'll squander up
some typical reply such as
helping the homeless
or inventing a cure for cancer

my life has no clear ambition

the only thing clear to me is my piss
after a few beers
I, however, want my writings to be clear
yet they're always vague

so maybe that's my life's ambition
to piss clear after writing a worthy poem

broken dishes

you seem to idle
yourself into fuzzy
corners
and sit there for days
on end
pupils sinking
minutes deranging
until God appears
before your virgin brow
touching you with
somber sin
and leaving you
to sort through
the dishes' sharp
porcelain which
lie in pieces
on the floor

Dublin blues

one last test
to tame a wild whim
days spent in coffee
pills, borderline atmosphere
paranoia
translating religion from ink
to soul and back again

I give myself over
and remain forgotten

I decided against tinker-boxes
lined with musical dancers
and cherry colored roses before
I knew you
instead, I await for cold sidewalk
prayers to allude me
crude, poverty-stricken images of
starvation and half-cracked poems
to portray me as a jester
to the harboring queen who
fills her crown in chardonnay
during queer moments
when her words mean more to her
and less to me

beyond the boredom which
strikes its sulphuric awakenings
in absolute awe
beyond the seas drowning itself
in meaningless pederasty
a muzzle of taxis carry me in pieces
to the four corners of the earth
I disperse and trickle into the
heavens

an image of you reflected in a moon beam
the quilt of quais and quaint

troubadours remains frayed and
this delayed plane ride in honor of you
remains restless and incompetent

I want you to know
how much I care
before I go

rain

I'm only an ounce
of sorrow divided into
millions of others

I fall onto you
and seep inside

I cry

Weep for the desert
and annihilate the filth
accumulated for ages
before I knew of you

I bend the trees
and rinse the streets
of disease
stinging songs in the winter
and soothing the summer conformity

letting loose in a cloud
and melting upwards
afterwards, into the
great divide
I smell of the cosmos
and taste as sweet
as a French red wine

I desire to be no more
than I am

feather'd Stars

I want to breathe in unison
with the pulse of a twirling
late autumn fleeting wind
and feel the moon crawling
beneath my skin

I want to regulate religion
within my veins
and calculate a cantos
onto a passing stranger

I want to rise with the sun
and repose with the stars
and read the last poem
of the last poet

when all is done and said
I want nothing more than
a cozy bed to let my
dreams loose on

the window way

they move the window way
over sleepy terrain with
blank books and dry pens

old lovers from the past
present lovers
and future ones as well

they're caught in a pink hell
where their riddle tossing's
become anorexic along
with their drooping teeth

I felt this coming
long before we
were borne

a soldier's poem

- for the absurdity of war

down with the chaos
down with the confusion
down with the drugs that
bind brothers together
and let us reap fields for
our golden master

my tears fall only
for those that have fallen
for themselves
and cast aside the cries
of a million children

I shed my blood for
wrinkled paper
and set my family's name
on fire for a commander
the chief

I'm bound for heaven this way

my bones decay beneath
a simple granite cross
and I'm remembered
through a folded flag

waiting for a download

does she remember midnight

lantern-lit lips

train station tragedy

assembling an orchestra
out of cigarette butts
and crushed velvet top hats

the audience
mute
stagnant
pale beneath a piano
downpour

a secret artist
behind the shadows
waving light in
their faces of dread

I find myself

describing my heart
with a banjo

wires sending souls
at various speeds

listen
I didn't mean
a cavity when
I folded the pages

only a bent book
with autograph

the crazy drunks
glued on the streets

I sober eye them
smile
carry-on
burn to ash

as they cry like
hammers with
straw nails

III

atop the Spire, looking down

Dublin ramblings

Talbot street musings

maybe you weren't real
so what's the big deal
if we lost our marbles
along the river

I spilt my drink and
caught a glimpse of
your silver ring

I pace the streets
smoking
talking to myself
not having anyone
yet having everyone

the other night we watched
this cat pour his heart
out on stage

I'm leaving tomorrow
its time to turn this
dog-eared page

a light thru a muddled glass

I sat in this hostel bed last night
and trembled
stomach full of Cajun chicken
and red wine
I longed for redemption and awoke

to find myself sleeping next to me

life is crazy

I lit a candle for you
on this cold and lonesome day
I prayed we would make it through
and if we didn't I prayed for
God to take care of you
I left the church and gave
2 euro to a bum
who promised me a blessed life
since then ive been to a few pubs
where I've pondered this mysterious life

drunk before dusk

the buses roll by
taxis slay the streets
the bums have had their drinks
and a mother walks by with her child
if I knew what to say
I would call you now
and apologize for my mistakes
do you want to hear
something I really fear
or do you wanna go your way

I believe in love

I believe in love

even in the face of

heartache and despair

she's a sexy beast

with vibrant wings

and gentle fingers laden

with sterling silver rings

I caught her on the bridge

of the Liffey

and let her go soon thereafter

I believe in love

even in the face of

heartache and despair

feelings afar

I keep walking

without a heart

I keep mumbling

quiet prayers alone

I feel our shadows

from 5,000 miles away

tears upon cathedral steps

I can taste more clearly
our demise poised on a simple
e-mail with the ending set to
"xxx"

I tried to sum it up
with a simple goodbye
and a parting tear
but that is never enough

no

we need drama
its human nature
to drag out the suffering

we'll feel better with
these tears and
soft parting hymns

art

keep on driving
down dark roads
dressed with fog and rain
pour your pain out
onto an empty canvas
spread your fears like watercolour
and watch them mix with joy
or better yet
have a beer or 10
and write a poem

art will lead
you home

its best to keep quiet

at times
until you can no longer
bear your own self-imposed silence
thus forcing your sweet soul
to explode upon a blank page

that's religion

that's art

Friday

singing this same ol'
free falling chorus
of loose letters and
bruised beats

no one is interested
in a song they've
never heard

its natural to turn
away from those
who need love

we all need it

were too scared to give it

too nervous to see our
own reflections in
our cracked mirrors

my pants are stained
with the paint used
to portray the
moment when beauty
bowed down to
the beast

hott

placing my gouache in

a porcelain bowl

adding water

dip with brush

and drip onto paper

that's like life

we give ourselves over

to the unknown

just free and alive

no guidelines

only organic movement

and a heart song

that's hott

inner-piece

and its trueee
that there is a light

nada fright
nor dead-heat plight

it waves from the cosmos
like a kite

it can find you
in a dream

something ya never seen

I cant say much else
about it

you'll see it
when it finds
its way
to youuu
!

trueee
!

peace to
inner self

and back

again

pennies and dimes

you want what I can't understand
an empty friend
a naked hand
someone to bind your fear
and faith together
and keep them in place
with dark-alley drugs
and rituals read at dawn
from writers who've ruined
my rest

you want salvation without redemption
free pennies and dimes
classy clothes and cheap rhymes
someone's eternal time

I thought I could fill your void
and make you mine
but I close my eyes and
you're nowhere inside

all you've left behind
are simple strands of hair
on my bed
and an empty head left
out in the rain to soak-up
this poison which falls
from sickly clouds

you are my light

with all of this confusion
in every day life
you betray me with a
charming illusion
you turn my day to night
and fill my dreams
with fear and fright

you are my light
and I will fight
to keep you burning
even tho a few may fall
in your steps
your overall goal
is one short of
universal redemption

with this world melting away
we need new hope to
guide us into a
new day
you told me you had to go
but I know you'll be ok
this town is too small
for my imagination
I wish I could write you
something to show my
eternal gratification

you are my light
and I will fight
to keep you burning
even tho a few may fall

in your steps
your overall goal
is one short of
universal oblivion

silence

things might
be easier
if you quit talking

let's fade into the past

my feelings of you
are not enough to last

 I wish they were

I wish you would open up
like in days of old
when we both faced the future
so brave, so bold
and never looked back

sometimes I retrace our footsteps
on a map and
shed a tear
knowing we were once here, there

I'm
nowhere

without you

dreaming like a symphony

the quiet
before the symphony
begins

its like meeting
a girl in a dream

and you know every
scene that's gonna
fold out like
the back of your hand

each moment plays out
in mute defiance

until the first violin
ushers in the
orchestra

and before you know it
the song
is over

and somehow
you always manage
to wake up
feeling refreshed

for Madeline Peyroux

I feel ya babe

days spent in the Paris metro

shedding your heart onto

guitar strings

no one understands

except for the few passer-bys

who toss a drunken hand of

2 euro

enough for a decent meal

and some inspiration to set into the

feel for a new song

feel it coming on

dawn breaking over Gare du Nord

one is never alone in Paris

as they look towards

their muse

about a Bukowski poem

I read this poem tonight
at the book store
by Charles Bukowski

he mentioned some great writer
who hung out with cool people
and drank beer
and told great stories
and wrote even greater
stories at home

then all of that hanging out
and beer drinking took
its toll upon the writer

and he aged too fast
and lost his will to write
and claimed that once
a writer loses the
will to write
its over

Sylvia Plath said the same
thing in 'The Bell Jar'
tho she wrote some
nice shit afterwards

I think that
once a person
loses the will to write
it finds its way
back to them in some
fashion or another

too bad I can't tell
that to Sylvia Plath

<u>snapshot Friday afternoon</u>

warm cup
of stale coffee
caught sitting
on the pot
for 2 long

toxic black
fumes from marker
fill my room
and leave my
head spinning

and this song
on my computer

an mp3
to set me
free

a dream
found in
eternity

untitledd

we ease our way onto

the scene like

a madman from a murder

mystery

glossy glances pierce

us from all

sidez

at lease we're

not in jail

take a breath

read your junk mail

there's something

good in

everything

!

Winter in Temple Bar

the solemn streets still
house our shadows
years after we walked them
hand-in-hand
as our eyes acted like
they had never been burned
by the sun before

I know I let you down
its hard for me to come around

we offered up our innocence
in the name of
mystery-love and a lie
rushing headlong into the night
with falling tears
and a quick goodbye

I dedicate this poem
to what was
and what could've been
I lay it gently in
my left palm and lift
a flame to its right side

thinking of you as
its ashes rise
towards the sky

when the time comes

let us go
go soft into the night
without looking back

we shall keep our eyes upon
this dimly lit path
and see ourselves
as ghoulish shadows
emerging from the dark
into the light
as angels dressed in
linen as pure as snow
and golden halos
which will reflect endlessly
through the halls
of heaven

Irish rain

its been a while
since I've seen that magic
in your colourful smile

its been a while
since we walked that mile
in the Dublin rain
freezing in the cold
exposing our pain

I've found its all the same

mile upon mile
heart upon heart
love finds you
in the light
and leaves you
weeping in the dark

golden time

everyone's happy
with their silver needles
and powder-puff'd pills
their pupils expand
like foreign lands
emerging from open oceans
of blueeee

parlez-vous the loving tongue?
or are you just another one
who is looking for
what can't be found

deaf to God
eagerly awaiting a sound
to resound in your
melting mind

we got our wine
we got our pills
we got our love

we're golden time

Valentine's day

its Valentine's day
and the girl I love
doesn't love me

no, she loves another
another closer to her home
closer to her heart

I drink alone
in the dark
while she roams the
streets alone with him
and touches a part
of him that
she once touched of mine

I'm fine
with my wine
on Valentine's day

who knew you were blue

its never easy
waking up in the middle of
the afternoon
with a fading dream you're
trying so hard to recapture
in 3-D

it always slides away
like love
like life

no matter how much you
cherish what you have
or what you want
you always want more

throwing up all of this
poetry into a toilet
after a night of heavy drinking

prose is sinking,
giving way to new words

she told me she wanted passion
yet her sense of fashion was cold
and they all said I was too old
for her child-like ways anyhow

her hands felt cold that night
I remember their touch quite well

touchdown

wow
its strange
admitting to
loving this cup
of stale coffee
I blame the recent
flu which crippled
my body
or the fact that its
8:30 AM Tuesday
morning
Satan himself
is still sleeping

its cool pondering
art techniques and travel
plans or marveling
at the fact that I've been
sober this long

I feel one with the
Holy Spirit which
lives in me
(it lives in you as well)

I've touched down and
I plan on staying
on the ground for
quite some time

hear my poem. hear my song

I'm coming to terms
with reality
I'm finished
(for now)
with pompous poems
and meandering metaphors

I'm aiming for simplicity

I wanna feel God's love
all day and all night
(when I say God
I mean Buddha
Allah
Mohammed
Oprah
etc...)

I wanna share
my findings with you
and remind everyone that
life is short
but love is long

hear my poem
hear my song
be true to yourself
be true to everyone else
and you'll find
that light to guide you
in the darkest of night

the heart's secret

its late at night
and I got them old feelings
of her and I
naked in bed
Dublin dark and
drunk like teenagers

I wonder if she has the
same thoughts

I wonder what her thoughts
circle around now
as I finish this
6-pack of Guinness

so much for
keeping clean

one day we'll
figure out what
this beating heart's
secret means

love (again)

we can't get enough
we come back for more
knowing the outcome

its like a drug

its love

watch it move
by your face
by your heart
without a wink

you're left naked
and don't know what
to think

take a drink
of water from
the sink
and wash her
cryptic kiss
down your
throat

then you're
safe to tote
her memory around
in a notebook
called
poetry
for a willing
eye
to
spy

herspace

I like Lauren's
poetry
its simple-like
full of love
and
when I read
it
I see a
white dove
soaring
across
my mind

peace

home

what's it feel like
to be felt like
a ghost

all alone

smooth and cold

pale and poor

remind me once more
why you chose to leave
and I'll leave
you alone

who wants poetry
who wants love
we're all empty
and sullen waiting
for our number
to be called

everyone is ready
to go home

on the edge

no more friends
they're foes
and I'm bipolar

will you love me
like this

or do I have
to be
like
that

St. Patrick's day

I imagine myself as Brendan Behan
locked up in a cold steel cell
Saturday night on St. Patrick's day

the pipes in the distance joyfully
find their way across the hills
to my lonesome ears
bringing back a world once
rich and vibrant, healthy to
my learning soul
now I'm left alone to bare these
words, faults and all
to a willing pair of eyes

I don't expect redemption
I won't go to church to find God
as I've found him once before
He always gets buried beneath
my sentient, shallow burdens
sins as some may say
I'd like to think of them
as remedies for a cruel, poisonous world

but oh, let me once more
pry open my shut eyes
and peer out of these bar'd windows
and watch the world melt by in all
of its simplistic beauty
like the turning of an hour glass
each second is short
yet each second is sweet

the pipes in the distance still carry-on
as a tear and partial smile
dress this solemn face

for a French bum

broken to bits
drunk as hell
muttering words
caught up in his
stale cigarette smoke

he finds eternity
as she guides him along
the riverside
hand-in-hand
she kisses him on the cheek
and lets him go

he wanders around the bookshop
thumbing through books with
an intense eye
never understanding the foreign word
but it feels good to him

he finds eternity
as she guides him along
the riverside
hand-in-hand
she kisses him on the cheek
and lets him go

with no more intuition
and no more money for
booze or books
he wanders around the
museum's heavily populated entrance
his smoke forms a loose figure
he stops and peers towards the open skies

he finds eternity
as she guides him along
the riverside
hand-in-hand
she kisses him on the cheek
and lets him go

hungoverhungryandhyperoncoffee

i a lazy reader

im a lazy writer 2

shortcuts and bad grammar
are the new grammar

the new art

a Picasso
with tints of DaVinci
and Basquiat brushstrokes
and Warhol advertisements

life is momentum
so is art
and its definition is
vague 'cause of
the momentum which carries
it from here
to there

everywhere is
motion

moving like
angel wings

our hearts sing
the song of
movement

even in sleep
we dream of
going and we don't
stop dreaming until
we wake up
then we're off again

death is momentum 2
who new?
God from above
carries our lil souls
to the other side
where tha dark shadows
hide in the corner
and we shine together
like one magnificent
masterpiece created by
a 3 year-old on a lite-brite

enough religion
people will get mad
not because (possibly) they hate
my god
but because they are sad
inside and have yet
to realize that my god
is their god
and their god
is your god
and now
I'll nod out
for un autre cup
of coffeeeee...!

my indie dealer

the putter of drowning rain

happiness sublime

new music that shines!

I'm a Pitchfork freak

and only discover new

indie bands there

emo

day-glo

hip-hop ambient

violins to charm

my evenings

unless I'm drinking

with Shane MacGowan

a grey Thursday over this lil town

remember dusk dawning over the old canal
the rooftops littered with dim lights
and the sparkle of the river
remember the words spoken which
dissolved into the air
and found their way again years later

we were reborn and died again
we were then and now
the past that married the present
and the future faded

we held a vision

quarrels in life's lay-out
take the good with the bad
and keep smiling, man
nothing is worth losing it all
even if all seems small
its just tiny pixels of a
huge picture in progress
coming into play day-in
and day-out
the end product will
take yer breath away

a real masterpiece
2 come

brothers and sisters

are we really what we are?
sinners searching for salvation
near and far?
to test fate time and time again
taking our chances and
never expecting an end
to our actions
that generally carry us in circles

some people think they know
what they're looking for
some say they found it
others, well, I don't know about them

I do know that we're all
in the same plane
and I'm not in the mood to
point fingers or name names
but we're all brothers and sisters
the pain you inflict upon me
is inflicted upon you
just like the sky and the sea
both share the same blue hue

so cheer up
what is sad now
never lasts forever
anyhow

my thoughts on writing

this writing has me
in stitches
its taken too
seriously
like a
lobotomy
or an organ
transplant
it should be more like
that feeling
one gets as a kid
entering a playground
for the first time
no rules
no stress
just fun
in the
sun

Brendan Behan's glass

Brendan Behan's glass
raises questions beyond anticipation
cries of joy in the streets
intoxicating irresponsibility
issues itself to me
as nuns raise their eyes to
a vacant cross

Brendan Behan's glass
corrupted an empty pub
where the tap ran dry
an old man cried in the corner
with no one to dry his tears
or soothe his fears of a coming
world where pubs go empty and
its occupants occupy offices
otherwise

Brendan Behan's glass
was once new and knew not
of being old or chipped
or dirty
like a baby growing up
into a well rounded man
seasoned in earthly knowledge
divine!
twisted by tales, learning ever
growing, going
far away from his inner light
like a bhikku forging sonnets
in the name of haiku

Brendan Behan's glass
full to the brim with
disease, disastrous words
made pretty
swimming to the brim
in women and words

every poet's passion
listening loosely for lust
but turning to dust instead
an evolving head
painted clean off its shoulders!

Brendan Behan's glass
an antiquity for collector's
not worth more than a penny
shined suspiciously on a Sunday
to me, if I could only be
like you and you be like me
oh, oh orgasmic soul vibrations
vivid surreal....sure

Brendan Behan's glass
prefers the mundane dipped
in LSD
wow
imagine that

Brendan Behan's glass
is empty
and the barman fills it for him
only to look up
and Brendan is
gone

cosmos

nude

white

an empty canvas
home to majestic memories
of the imagination

a piano sonata dances
upon the bleak surface
leaving a trail of melodies
behind

your taxes
which add up dollar
onto dollar
penny onto
penny

monetary values that follow
us in death

at least that's what
we're to believe
as we count the stars
wondering exactly how
far they stretch
into the cosmos

I'm

an
open book
reciting passages
from the past
I know each
l
by heart
I recite them
in the dark
and re
arrange the letters
2 form
broken
sent
ences
I
m

p
 o
  e
   t
    r
    y

in the mirror

nothing is as it ever seems
as you look into your mirror
the reflection is not of you
but a ghost who gave itself
over to the wrong odds
pale and slender
laden with razor blades which
cut every thought before its
borne into something special
your nerves are left exposed
and the pain is familiar
you feel nothing
nothing
nothing to keep you alive
nothing left inside
but you thrive on a string
of salvation planted in your
heart as a child
gazing into the mirror
a small smile forms
and the feeling of
victory rises within

rise from the ashes

we live with this disease
we feed it with federal pills
and wonder why it continues to grow
we carry our burdens out in the open
showing them off like a new pair of shoes
we claim to be where its at
while we're really
lost out in the wilderness
wandering thru pacts of
wild beasts

when we give in
when we rise
when we burn the demons
with their own flame
we rise again like
a phoenix out of the ashes
of our past lives

nirvana never negotiates
death never dreams
only our shadows remain
on the rolling plains
of conscious reality
left alone to feed on memories
of love

I love the way my shadow
dances with yours

this is eternity
beneath a bleeding sun
at night the moon will reign
reciting poetry for our
hungry hearts

inspiring inspiration (the art of writing lost then found)

we spread into each moment
of day, drumming out a beat
as we go along
tap
tap-rat
tap-rata-pat-tap
moments splatter
into moments
memories fade
and the future unfolds
golden gaiety forgotten
or so we think
until it ushers its
charming way into us
once more
and we head for the door
ready to go out into the world
and show the world
what we've got!
its art
and art is love
love is lust
distilled in memories
of that past
present, future
and the time beyond
time which carries itself
soft into the unknown
let the words
be words
let them work
their magik
let them find their

way thru your soul
plant them in your soil
watch them grow

bleed on baby
we know you're there

rushing into the dark

with her cold lipped freedom
and her mystery stares
her meticulous femdom
and her mother-like cares
she holds her world tightly
in pale hands
coming on to me knowingly
exposing me where I stand

with her inquisitive inklings
pushing me near
and her prophecies sinking
I wonder what she fears
she never knows when to stop
she rambles on til dawn
doesn't know what she's got
she walks by like a flashy fawn

I sprinkle these stale words
on her hiding heart
she slices them into perfect thirds
dispersing them drunkenly in the dark
she's got me by my strings
as I dance like a mean marionette
she thinks thoroughly back on these things
and like an old fool, I haven't surfaced yet

how it grows in the evening and withers by the morn

where are you going dear lady?
do I not stir the flame which
flickers beneath your trembling bosom?
have our words yet transcended the norm
into that realm of radical romanticism?

the clock ticks out
moment upon moment
and grows darker
the shadow of your figure
hides a delicate surprise
of gentle caress
the touch of your lips
will never allow me to forget

can we continue this show for a little longer
perhaps until dusk turns to dawn
and the birds awaken to sing us
their song of
love fleeing

I saw Love

I saw Love
and looked her in the eyes
beauty brought back from the past
riddled deep in new skin
her voice spoke softly of then
as her lips laughed in the present
and her heart longed for the future

I saw Love
in front of my face
I pushed aside the anxiety of knowing
perfection had presented itself
unto me
and stood in the moment, dazed with delight
what can you say to Love
that she has not heard before?
the silence spoke louder than any syllable
as we savoured the moment which passed as quickly
as it was borne

I walked away with an image of her smile
and diamond eyes cutting thru reality
exposing a dream beneath the surface

to-do list

go to the post office and mail
the Wilco tickets I sold on eBay

cash in some money orders at the bank
go to Wal-Mart and buy a frame for a poster

swing by Whole Foods to buy health food
I'm on another health kick which
will last longer this time
for real

go to an art store and buy a
watercolour journal
do these exist?

come home
write a poem
and visit with sister and nephews
who are coming over for super

walk down to the river with the oldest nephew
and search for 4-leaf clovers
take the dog along
and everyone's happy

Tuesday is the new Sunday
the day for rest and fun
how would our lives be if
God finished his work on Tuesday?
not much different I suppose

when evening rolls around
go to the bookstore with Steven
buy coffee and talk

browse thru the cheap books
for artistic inspiration
aka, stealing ideas

come home and talk online
ease the strain of life
over the walls of the inner-net

light my candle and think of Proust
its night time after all

perhaps paint a new picture before bed
Henry Miller would be proud
as the colours dripped
and ran into one another
like a song seeping into a soul
its the magic known as art
the magic that finds its way
into our hearts
the magic that makes the world's wheels
spin 'round and 'round
and makes gravity push down to help keep
our meek selves on the ground

time to go
I'm not going to get anything done
typing away behind this PC

to the guy on the scooter

he rode up on his scooter
and I was struck by the
absurdity of his mustache
"when can I get the 10 dollar
manicure and free drink?"
he briskly remarked with
a look of goofy innocence
plastered upon his face
we all looked at him
and shrugged our shoulders
"thanks a lot for the help!"
he replied as he took off
his helmet and went into the bar
after a few more smokes and
stories were shared between us outside
he exited the bar with a smug grin
which took the place of his
previously silly facial expression
"Wednesday at 5!" he joyously shouted
as he hoped back onto that scooter
and rode off into the Manhattan night

the painted man

he drew himself onto a canvas and wondered when he would get out. he ended up over seas in search of a girl who broke his banjo. he'd stay up late with her, watching steering wheels and foliage unite, strumming that banjo like Doc Boggs. his voice fractured every recollection her heart could recite. they'd weep together then make fake love. its what they knew. love lingered in the air but never once crossed their minds, for he was too busy picking that banjo to notice and she was occupied in her own tears of childhood bliss. then one day when the moon rose in place of the sun, she said she was done and hit the banjo with a hammer sent to her from Portugal by some heroin hero of the day. the banjo shattered like a dove if doves could shatter and the patter of rain resembled the orchestra from some depressing opera.

he painted onto that canvas more frantically now. vivid colors, black and white clashing with red and blue. her demented tears started falling once more, much to her unaware, frayed mind. the hours passed and her tears flooded their quaint dwelling, washing the man away along with the colors of his paintings. he ended up back home where his canvas was no longer recognized. the city's mayor saw him float in and ordered to have him arrested. "this filth won't stand," he shouted, "by God, someone arrest this man!" he was taken into custody and slept in a locked cell. he gazed at the bars and painted them with his imagination much reminiscent to Ken Kesey's trippy bus, swirls and twirls of colors. this made him happy and he decided to repaint himself that night. in the morning, the mayor came by to show his tobacco ridden teeth and cholesterol cluttered heart to the washed-in, unpainted man but upon arriving to the cell,

the mayor was struck fiercely by a unique sight of discharmed colors and side-tracked shading..2 year old lines and poetic rhymes scrawled all over the man's canvas and cell. "what the hell?" sang the mayor as a shattered dove emerged from the man's latrine. it was the most beautiful painting the mayor had ever seen. he demanded the prisoner be let go. 2 and a half seconds later, the mayor died from that aforementioned cholesterol problem. the man kissed his stiff hand and left the jail with an upside-down frown.

the man entered the subway and caught the first train, not knowing where it went.
the clicking and ticking of a passenger's watch brought upon déjà-vu for the newly painted man. he got off at the next stop, tossing a dollar to the passenger and headed up toward the street. the street was empty except for a plane missing a wing. a drunken pilot sat in the seat staring into the controls. "I'm almost there," he mumbled time and time again. the man shook the pilot out of his stupor and explained, "I'm here like you, we are like the rain, shake this silly hand and take me back to my banjo-breaking dame." the pilot looked at him with sober sincerity. "yes, dear sir," the pilot said, "I'm missing a wing but if you sing me a Barbra Streisand ballad, we can do this." the man cleared his throat and proceeded to sing. the plane started up and took off and in roughly an hour, or 5 minutes, later, the man was back in the

land of his gal. he shook hands with the pilot as the pilot started up the plane. "good luck, dear sir, your voice was lovely." "the sun is David Hasslehoff," the man replied as they waved goodbye to each other. after an hour of walking the desolate streets, the man came across a headstone placed beside a parking meter with the words, "drowned by her own tears" scrawled in lipstick upon the cold granite. the man knew that that was his girl even tho it never mentioned her name. not knowing what to do, or where to go, he looked up towards the moon and began to sing that Barbra Streisand song again.

zombies out for raw flesh

sitting up until dawn
thinking and blinking
sleep won't come
yet morning dreams feather
me down with anticipation
of a coming world clean
with new scenes
time out
its not suppose to be like this
buy a bag and destroy the evidence

make yourself you again

it all goes down like this
and comes back up like that
no one is watching
for their eyes have been
gouged out by bloody needles
and spoon-sugared flames have fried
their nervous nerves
they dress the nighttime streets
like zombies out for raw flesh
and I find myself tagging along
the devil on my left shoulder says
"take this and feel that!"
while the angel on the right says
"you know this is wrong
sing them a song"
but the song won't come
so I follow along
like a zombie out for raw flesh

sleepless in NYC

everything is like it is
you say you can see
if that's the truth then why
do you need me
you want lust without love
friendship with no feelings
I'm bruised and beaten
and you laugh from your home
far away over the sea
I wish you could see me
see what you've done
I've never felt worse but I feel
better than I ever have before

lonely nights in New York City
are never really lonely
there's always a lone soul
drinking their minutes away
drink over drink
smoke over smoke
I wish I could roam around in their heads
see through their bloodshot eyes
and crawl into their cold beds
as dawn once again claims the day

but this is not how it is
yet this is how it is
everything is confusion
and confusion is clarity
like the clear ice which melts
in your summertime glass

another day dies down

as the sun dances from one end
of the sky to the next
can love be love when every word
spoken was a lie

can feelings find their way
thru a muzzled glass

can a voice be heard over
a crying moon

sleepless night in New York City

sleepless now
and forever more

her eyes

her eyes collected the meticulous
mystery of the dance
the warm neon
the soft smoke
the tender flesh she caressed
with her imagination

she wanted them
like this
or like that

it's hard to tell how
green her hell had become

the angels, angled on high
had cracked the sky with
piercing eyes
exclaiming the Word thru
jolts and bolts of
sweet saxophone

come on, little girl
it's time to go home
take your element of desire
and weave me a web of tangible fire

wine and postcards

who's you?

where to?

nice to see you!

why not blue?

a girl selling Jim Morrison

postcards and t-shirts

outside of Pere Lachaise

cemetery

I mad-luv-lust eye her

and carry-on towards

the end of the line

where we'll all dine

with the finest wine

in due time

physics of the mind/ heart

tell me like before
you told me before
how things went in your head
I know you lie
the devil's in your heart and
he's hungry as fuck
for gullible words and virgin fears
bleeding hearts and quaint genitals
I dressed you up as saint in disguise
to hide the fire which raged behind your eyes
if I couldn't see it, it wasn't there
but that's not the case and now I'm being punished
I called out at the wrong time, grabbed the wrong hand
like a lonely soldier left wounded in a foreign land

I'm twisted with toxic fumes left whirling in my skull
of drugs, dark love and absinthe alcohol
finding inspiration is hard when its been stolen away like a child
how can I hate someone so much that once made me smile
it's not fair for you and it ain't fair for me
I respect you enough to tell you that one day we'll all be set free
but the bitter words which rolled off your tongue still linger
next to your poison deceit and confused mind
you walk this world lead by your lust, still you are blind
open your eyes to see that it just ain't me

cold, cold, cold heart

she proceeded to show the
slow winter which had
formed upon her lips
the frost which dangled at the tips
were a unique feature
she got this way when
she least expected it
some say a night's unexpected dream
had unlocked her convicted heart
and the reality of the neglected
years had flooded its flimsy walls
sending her grasping and fighting
for that familiar foreign truth she
was comfortable with

I saw her once again some years later
and the flame in her eyes had been replaced
with sharp icicles deadly enough
to puncture even the strongest man's
calloused heart
I smiled and walked away as she stared
off into the receding distance
with a bitter look frozen to
her blue plastic face

only if you could imagine

only if you could imagine
a world gone wrong
the dirt has stained my shirt
as I crawled thru the valleys
in search of the crown
you dropped on your way down

only if you could imagine
the soul you left sinking
struggling for air in the ocean
only a quick notion would suffice
to stop this drowning
so roll the dice

take a chance
learn to live

only if you could imagine
a letter penned from an inmate
speaking of God's undying love
laced with tear stains

a fond goodbye

only if you could imagine

be what you are

can you be yourself
without shaking it to the fear
accumulated in your head
from memories of what you were

be what you are
and love what you've become
blossom slowly, beautifully into the years
like a delicate wildflower in a barren field
be what you are
let the truth seep thru
and shine

as we gather together
in cozy pads, drinking expensive wine
discussing a long gone time
enjoying this now without mentioning it

wow

look at what we've become

honey

the corporate smack
is the world's worst crack
it hooks you as a kid
gives ya false security
a peppermint home
hindered with honey
dripping from the end of the needle
until every little
piece is gone

and with nothing left to do
you gaze inside your cold turkey mirror
eying yourself like a caged animal
that's no longer part of this petting zoo

full throttle

she waits in time
shy and sublime
beating decadence with platinum blonde hair
and ghost-like sick skin
dressed with style
and a new pack of cigarettes
camel menthol lights

some things never change
the flash in her eyes ain't the same
deep and sunken, swimming in decay

she's still the American queen
the hippest chick I've ever seen
lusting it out, full throttle
lost in the bottle
I'd pull her out but I'd fall in
instead I sacrifice her
for the reality I radiate in

the shit we do while young
and restless, never ending drama which
twists and twirls us around and around
like a wild tornado on urban land

I'm an old bhikku
who's been you
its just a passing phase

live it out
drink it out
shoot it out
come clean
get dirty

love
love
love

its God's greatest
drug

the creation of all things

the creation of all things
sinister in its lifestyle
lovely nonetheless

madness in the mirror
as I watch her undress
a distressed voyeur
of digital regress

the world inside
is just as dark as
the world outside

she mumbles some words
Beauty falls before her as her
Arabic lips waltz

the creation of all things
lustful in its lifestyle
organic down to the climax
then up again

take it easy

we gotta take it easy, babe
we gotta bring it to the light
we gotta expose everything, babe
then we'll feel alright

every time we get like this
temptation takes our troubles to the grave
only to re-expose them sometime later
discovering that we weren't so brave

so take it easy, babe
remember these hard times
trying to find a friend amongst foes
selling your dollar to buy a dime

and when you're looking for that word
to hook your melody
I'll be your rhyme
only if you can promise me
an easy going mind
and to clear me off the slate
that I fucked up long ago
I'm not asking for forgiveness
I'm just wishing you wouldn't go

so take it easy, babe
we'll find each other again one day
and I'll be here
taking it easy, dear
writing poems alone with my beer

a little gospel goodness...yea

there were many years
I walked alone
down streets paved with sin
city lights, whiskey and women to do me in
I always thought my way was set
hell bound with a grin
and not a single regret
until the plagues of these pleasures
turned uglier each day
I sat up each morning and night
trembling, with not a word to say
until the Lord knocked a little louder
at my heart of stone
saying softly, "Son, its time to come home."
it was then I felt the Devil in each earthly vice
no longer would I have to roll the dice
'cause I knew I'd always be a winner with the Lord

truth

have I gone too far?
fallen off the edge while looking
down for something I dropped
is it possible to think about the past
without present bias?

I lift these words
from the holy book
its the only thing in life
full of truth

it breaks this free fall
and builds me a foundation
of rock where sand once collected

"what is truth?"

Pontius Pilate asked to Jesus
before having him sent to the cross

truth is the light you find
in a room encompassed with darkness
truth is an undeserved gift
much like grace
that fills the void within
if we just let go and allow it to

toxxxic terror

cold and toxic
laced with fear and dread
of impending destruction

flashes of light
depressed, agitated
frame of soul

the book of Revelation playing
out in my one man spirit
I let the beast in
now I'll usher him out
with brute independence
a taste of his own vomit

God swims in
thru the ocean
of withdrawal
to carry me back
home

the unsure disconnect

the unsure disconnect
unknown voices over the phone
catching up on old times

the airport, a ghost and a graveyard
with one million angels singing

as Satan searches thru
the debris for something
to salvage

cold tea and a warm memory

nobody is left outside
they've made their way indoors
safe from the snow
which sparkles on their sleeves

they wait like angels
with heavy halos
lit inches from their brains
yet they don't know what to think

you've washed your words down the kitchen sink
along with the alcohol which made you who you are
and though you write to me now
you wait far out in your haven where the wind doesn't howl
where the rain isn't wet
where the sun doesn't burn
yet you yearn for a healthy heir to deconstruct your deeds
set forth in valor one empty night

to remind you of the trees
and the apocalyptic hymns borne
from the sound of the wind
rushing thru the leaves

to lock the chains which
bound you to memories
some may call love
but you know them as nostalgic nuances

to set free your soul
in a labyrinth of mindless
propaganda called prose
which sprinkles your brow
in the midnight hour

when your memories begin to expire from the aging years
and your words are sent whirling around a drain
and your name shines like a plane receding off into the night

you're left with eternity, skies and seas
and a blazing sun which brings you back to life

Dali deformations

some recall themselves as feathers
floating freely with an electric pulse
I see them as forgers
fighting for fabled feminist forgiveness
only they're too childish to forgive themselves
and so they sit, with pompous teeth set towards tomorrow
with open eyes as to say,
"hey, take me in, friend."

alas, the coffee has grown pale
the smoke from the cigarettes has ceased to rise
and the poetry in your eyes is but a tiny
reflection of the sugar-soul you once possessed
some would venture to say you're still sweet
only the seasoned would see thru those lies
to find a real you
looking like a drunken Dali deformation

who are you
I ask myself this all the time
I'd be better off throwing my words out the window
and watch them fall
fall
fall
towards an uncertain end
an end to stop what you began
and an end to begin what
must start again

a dozen donuts

watch how she moves
how she grooves so spontaneously
without even meaning to do so
she's slick like the breeze
and fast on her knees
her reasons always rhyme
she bursts upon a scene
with no fear for the time
she's as hot as the summer pavement
beneath her busy feet
compare her to a dozen donuts
and you'll find she's just as sweet

embroidered empathy

light me up like a fist

crashing thru a wedding cake

the figurine on top tumbles

down and your frown falls to the ground

where I sew it neatly to a frayed edge

it was your grandmother's gown

now its just a piece of time

measured in stitches and fabric fading

embroidered empathy for a season gone wrong

light me up like a quicksilver moon

to which we toast expensive champagne to

the ascent of angels towards perfect poverty

the rags and filth you spoke life into

the dirt and disease of it all

it makes me laugh

another let down

just another put down
another let down
a long-lost veteran
of this 2 car town
drinking another beer
then another
throw in some wine
c'mon girl
gimme a sign
I'll craft your beauty
into a poem
so the kids you have
with that man I couldn't be
can read them
set them free
from their imposed misery
I'll be their hero
with dashing looks
and sexy books
then one day they'll see
that I'm just like them
and they're just like me

<u>golden bricks</u>

the faces staring at me

from the darkened theatre

mute and sick

with hollow cheeks

and sunken eyes

they're waiting for me

to make my move

show 'em what I got

but I cop out at times

like this

leaving them in disappointment

as I run away

arms full of golden bricks

smiling as I head

for the bank

condescending greatness

the way you see your
fleeting world
thru eyes of terror
catching every hawk
and turning them into vultures
to gnaw at the flesh you
stabbed with bitter words
the way you move like
Satan's shadow over the
fire-lined pits of Hell
burning fear into your
child's soft eye
laughing as she cries
living as she dies
with tar and nicotine falling
out of your decaying teeth
upon the floor you burn
with your wicked feet
the horns rising roughly
out of your cancer'd head
you spread yourself like
a disease after taking
frightened souls without
even saying please
you torture them with love
cut out their ambitions and
unleash a white dove

you work in the name of peace
you work in the name of wisdom
you work in the name of passion
you work in the name of perjury everlasting

you're Lucifer himself leading your followers
down rusty streets that haven't seen grace for years
everyone who goes against you lives in sorrowful fear
some follow their hearts to that welcomed end
others stab their genitals, proclaiming to be your friend

I go against the tide, I'm on my own side
sitting in a cloud, building up my pride
for that day that is soon to come
when God reaches down and places His
electric hand upon your heated head
exclaiming, "what is done is done"

work+bills=life

pourin' out every ounce of
worthless knowledge accumulated in your life
in the name of effort, urgency, work
I call it stupidity
I was watching a late night talk show last night
with Jeff Goldblum and really dug his voice
the way he compared the distance between our bodies
and the molecules within us to the distance
between stars
"we're really nothing," he said
and "life is a dream," he musta been reading Kerouac
the host asked if he had been taking drugs and
he lit an imaginary joint
but back to the point of nothing
and how we slave ourselves into crescent caskets
all for the vain venom of eccentric goals
set forth by goofy guys in gnarly white wigs
wielding feather'd pens

follow that mighty dollar, baby
and make me a man with a plan!
big cigars and gel'd hair slicked back, Jack
take a ride in my Cadillac
Bob Dylan is advertising Cadillacs now
he's got the idea right
if they give, take and take, its alright
but he's beyond these words, transcended
into the tapestry of heaven's silver window

I'm not sure where I'm going with this poem
maybe just trying to dissect life's complexities
and convince myself how simplistic it could all be
if we all just got on the same page
but, honestly, we're all content with our deadlines
taxes, 12 packs of beer and fancy clothes
soon we'll wake up to the Golden Eternity and
realize what we've really got

before I knew me

these memories are sexy
fallen and faded
nude with alcohol tongue
dressed like the rest
except new mind
Arabic kind
childhood lost
sexual desires found in
its colourful place
now dark and mildewed
with the rolling years

you called me out
before I knew me

I have a gun
loaded with verbs
if you don't run now
I will shoot your adjectives

you better watch it, baby
these pronouns don't lie

240

the current state of poetry

all of this poetry
is too depressing
its like a crucifixion of
the arts
what's in it for us
do we need saving
art was borne to show
us an easier way
then we curse it like
ungrateful dogs
(grateful gods)
blink our thoughts
then lick our muses
with tongues of hepatitis and honey
its a toast to divinity
and I don't have any wine

l'absinthe

what you
green hue
swarming seductions
amplified accusations
over fire burn't sugar
spooning ourselves out
infinitely over
again

goodness gracious
what ballz of fire
falling to the floor
"shit, you're gonna
burn the place down!"
stir it up
and take it in
quick
do another
it gets sweeter
I can see it
burn down yr
silken chest

demon dancing within
and wait for
the morning feel to
settle over eggs
and coffee

panik attack'd

it comes over you
that second in the mirror
where it turns silver
becoming critically conscious
of yourself in negative manifestations
of dreams folding to nightmares
and your heart starts thumpin'
wildly along with rabid recollections
of childhood drama
rejected sexual sins
prayer pushed painfully
down slippery steps

you've cornered yourself again
and there's no way out
expect to push yourself thru
the tears and pellets of sweat
which come rollin' down your
splittin' forehead

death seems better now than ever

you've gotta run
run
run
run
but there's no place 2 go
the world's a circle and
you're just chasing this demon
over and
over and
over again

light up a cigarette
put on Johnny Cash
the broken bass of his voice
singing Christ calms your
racing heart

inhale smoke
exhale peace
watch it float past
your fears
weaving webs of comfort for
you to let these demons
out upon
and it ends

and you feel safe
like a refugee landing on
freedom's sand
even tho you're standing on
pins and needles never
knowing when it'll
begin again

the end

he says he feels better
when sober
after the withdrawal stops
and he's left with
golden sunrays to brighten
his day

temptation teases his senses
once and awhile
til he caves in
buys a bag
and smiles
that sinister smile
of a junkie fixin'
his fix

its like this
but the conservatives
say its like that
the liberals are
lost in the woods

he admires her will to
quit the shit
tho he knows its
short lived
like their fairy book
romance
or the chance they
sold for more
blow

Satan laughs below
as the angels nod their heads

its times like this when he
would feel better being dead
what keeps a guy like
this rolling

his keen observations exploding

denoting existence
down to its
last
sentence

or just the hope
for another chance
to chance it all
away again

the end

set for seduction

a world like then
frozen stiff with war
beaming from a bubbled television
smitten vision of her
the virgin Mary
set for seduction

her brush strokes
gentle workings
wonderings of when
she's then, now
forever more

see it thru
rose colored glasses
express it with acoustic
aire, coasting notes floating
on high, bird lost in sky

to live like this
to die
to never fear
to be by her side

oils and acrylics now
dried, died, lied
prolly cracked with
running years
fears fought in pill bottles
soaring heart, wicked melody
"du-du-du-du-du-du..."
awake in bliss to
feel it all out

only to melt into night
disfigured faces, seething
colours, lite feet
flying!
watch them words, girl

and stop crying
I'll wipe the tears
with your magic hammock
hippie-flowered-forgetting day
speak nothing to say
and slip away to
evening's sleep

Index of titles in alphabetical order:

249

254